The Great Northern Women Colouring Book

Written & Illustrated by Diana Matos Gagic

**First published in 2019,
by Crafty Birdie Designs**

Text copyright © Diana Gagic, 2019
Illustrations copyright © Diana Gagic, 2019

Design for print by
Fullstop Studio

Edited by
Emma Turner

Created in Yorkshire

The moral right of Diana Gagic to be identified as the author and illustrator
of this work has been asserted in accordance with Sections 77 and 78
of the Copyright, Designs and Patents Act 1988.

All rights reserved. No part of this book may be reproduced, transmitted or stored in any form
or by any means, graphic, electronic or mechanical, including photocopying, taping
and recording, without prior written permission from the publisher.

Email: craftybirdies@gmail.com
Etsy: CraftyBirdieDesigns

Printed in England

ISBN 978-1-9160072-3-9

This book has been made with responsibly sourced uncoated paper (and love) and is suitable for colouring in using pens, pencils or crayons of your choosing... so feel free to be as creative as you like!

About the Author / Illustrator

Diana has lived for many years in the beautiful, historic Yorkshire village of Haworth, home to the famous Brontë sisters during the Victorian era. Like the Brontës, Diana loved to draw and create as a young girl, and remains passionate about art, nature, literature and equality. This hand-illustrated book has been created to help keep alive the memory of the great, pioneering women of Northern England and, hopefully, will inspire new generations to strive fearlessly for their aspirations - whatever they may be.

Great Northern Women

Celebrating a powerhouse of pioneering women in the 'herstory' of the North of England. Its musicians, artists, pilots, politicians, writers, scientists, businesswomen, sportswomen, activists, innovators and mould breakers, some you've heard of, and some you haven't. You may know of Anne Lister, the Brontë sisters and Britain's first astronaut Helen Sharman, but some names are less well known, such as Liverpudlian Olympic swimmer Hilda James who introduced the front crawl to the UK or Lilian Bader (also from Liverpool), who was the first known Black woman to join the RAF.

Amy Johnson

(1903 - 1941)

Amy Johnson CBE, from Hull, became the first British female pilot to obtain a ground engineer's "C" licence and initially became famous through her endeavour to set a record for a solo flight from London to Darwin, Australia. She was introduced to flying as a hobby, gaining an aviator's certificate and a pilot's "A" Licence in 1929.

Helen Sharman

(b. 1963)

Helen Sharman OBE, was born in Sheffield, and went on to become the first British astronaut and the first woman to visit the Mir space station in May 1991. Helen had the right scientific and educational credentials with her Chemistry BSc degree, PhD, and work experience as a Chemist to respond to a radio advertisement asking for suitable applicants to be the first British space explorer. Helen was selected for the Project Juno mission live on television, ahead of nearly 13,000 other adventurous applicants and has since received a star on the Sheffield Walk of Fame!

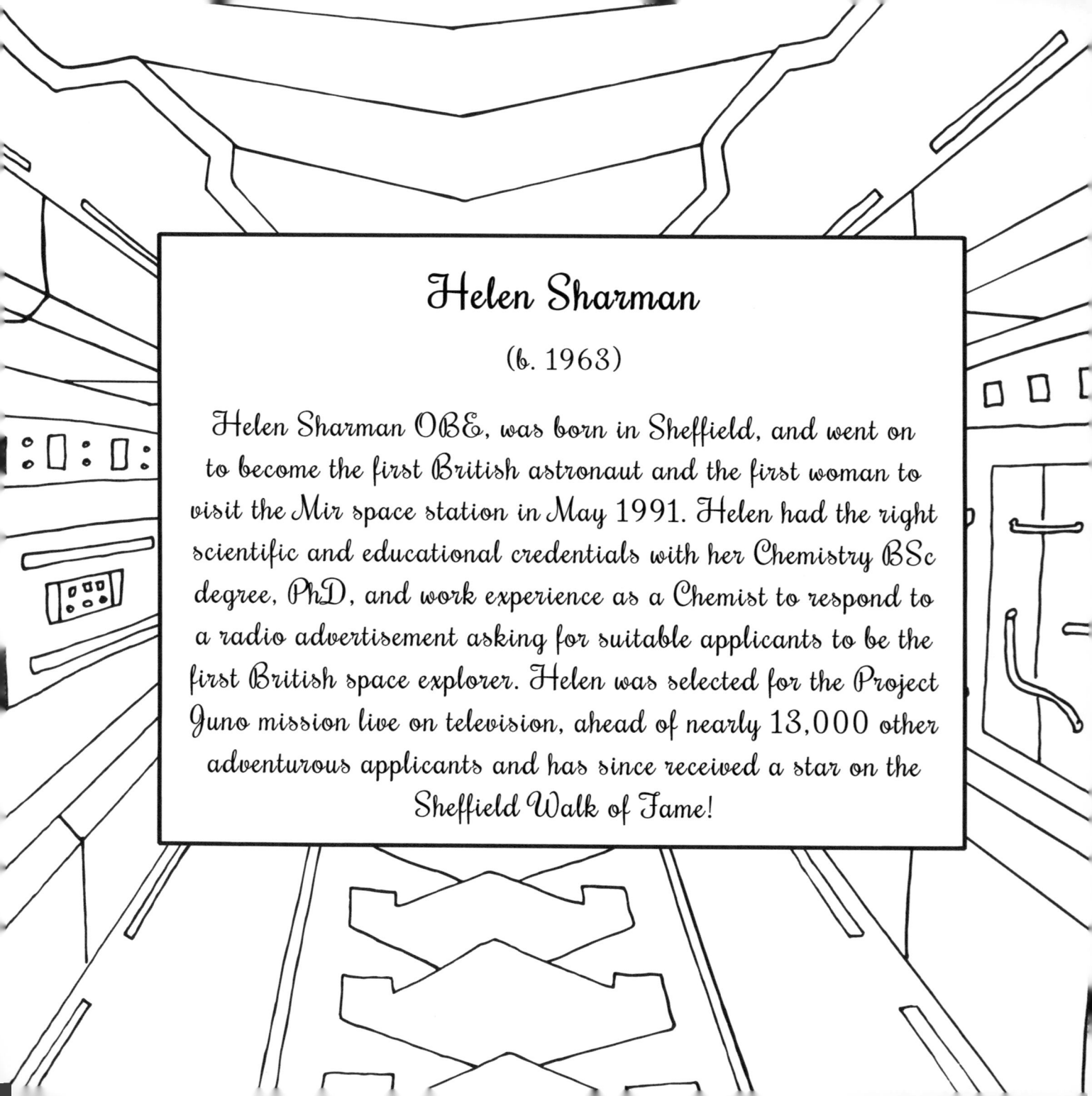

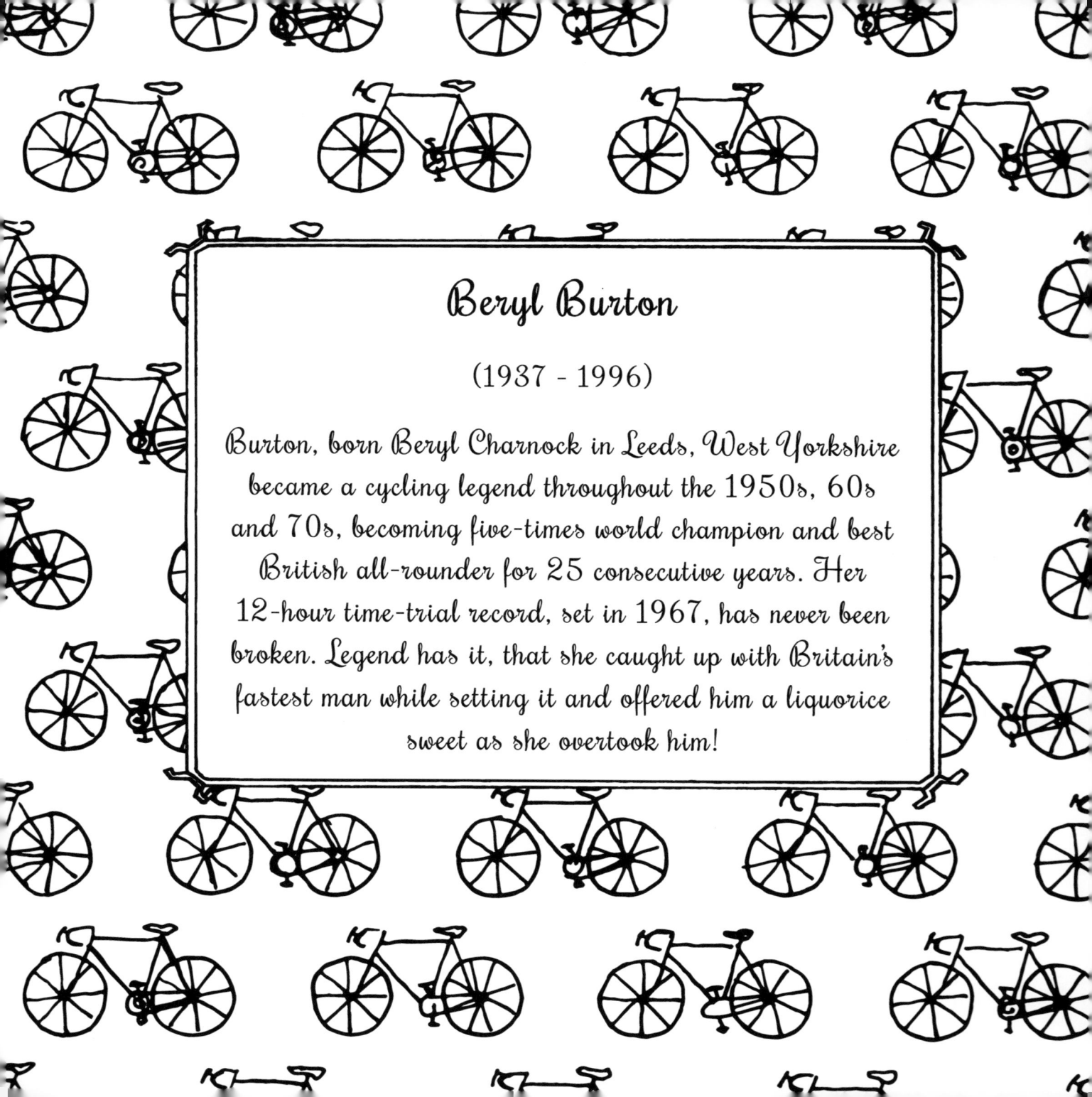

Beryl Burton

(1937 - 1996)

Burton, born Beryl Charnock in Leeds, West Yorkshire became a cycling legend throughout the 1950s, 60s and 70s, becoming five-times world champion and best British all-rounder for 25 consecutive years. Her 12-hour time-trial record, set in 1967, has never been broken. Legend has it, that she caught up with Britain's fastest man while setting it and offered him a liquorice sweet as she overtook him!

The Brontë Sisters

Charlotte, Emily and Anne were Victorian novelists who resided in the bleak but beautiful West Yorkshire village of Haworth. In their short lifetimes they fearlessly created works which are now widely accepted as classic masterpieces of literature. They succeeded in publishing some of the first feminist novels within a world dominated by male authors by using the pseudonyms of; Currer, Ellis, and Acton Bell.

Ellen Wilkinson

(1891 - 1947)

"Red Ellen" Wilkinson was a trade unionist, politician and writer from Manchester, who served as the first female Labour MP for Middlesborough East, Chair of the Labour Party and was Minister of Education. She became a national figure when she played a prominent role in the 1936 Jarrow Crusade in which the town's unemployed marched 300 miles to London to protest against extreme poverty within the north-east of England. The March provided an iconic image that helped to reform attitudes to social injustice and unemployment rights following the Second World War.

Anne Lister

(1791 - 1840)

Anne Lister was a business woman, landowner and diarist from Halifax, West Yorkshire. Throughout her life she kept detailed diaries where her most private thoughts were written in her own secret code. Lister meticulously chronicled all matters of her daily life including her love interests, her industrial activities, her financial concerns and her work improving Shibden Hall. She suffered harassment for her sexuality and was called "Gentleman Jack" by the residents in her home town. Despite this, Lister knew her own heart and was self assured enough to lead a lesbian lifestyle during strictly conventional Victorian times.

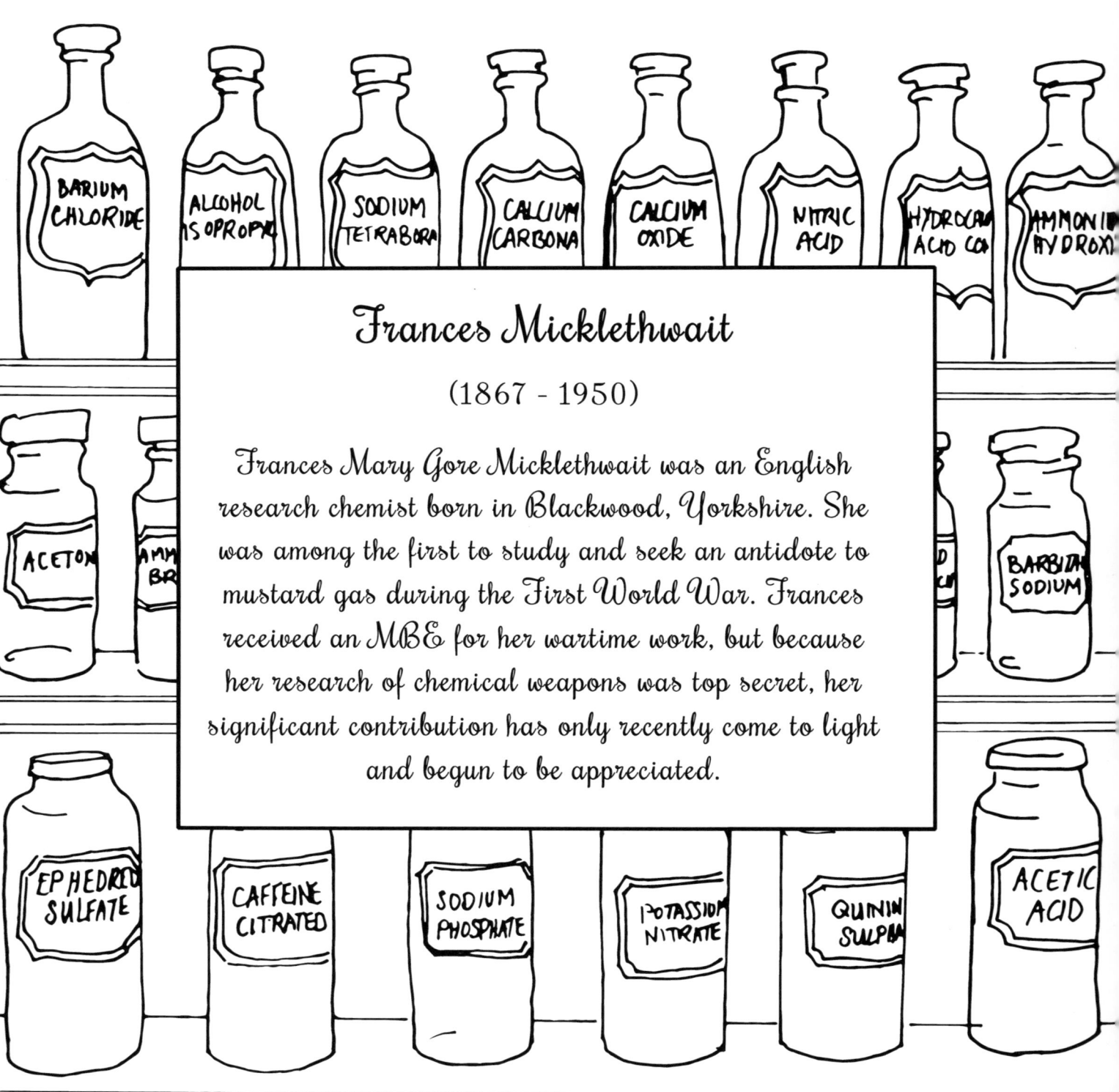

Frances Micklethwait

(1867 - 1950)

Frances Mary Gore Micklethwait was an English research chemist born in Blackwood, Yorkshire. She was among the first to study and seek an antidote to mustard gas during the First World War. Frances received an MBE for her wartime work, but because her research of chemical weapons was top secret, her significant contribution has only recently come to light and begun to be appreciated.

Hilda James

(1904 - 1982)

As an 11-year old Liverpudlian, Hilda began swimming to avoid Religious Education classes which went against her parents' beliefs. At 16 she had become Britain's best female swimmer and competed at the 1920 Olympics, where she helped win a silver medal in the freestyle relay. After further training in the US, she brought the front crawl back to the UK earning herself the nickname 'The English Comet'. In 1924 Hilda held every British and European freestyle record and several world records and again easily qualified for the 1924 Olympic team but her parents refused to let her go unchaperoned aged under 21 and she regretfully missed it!

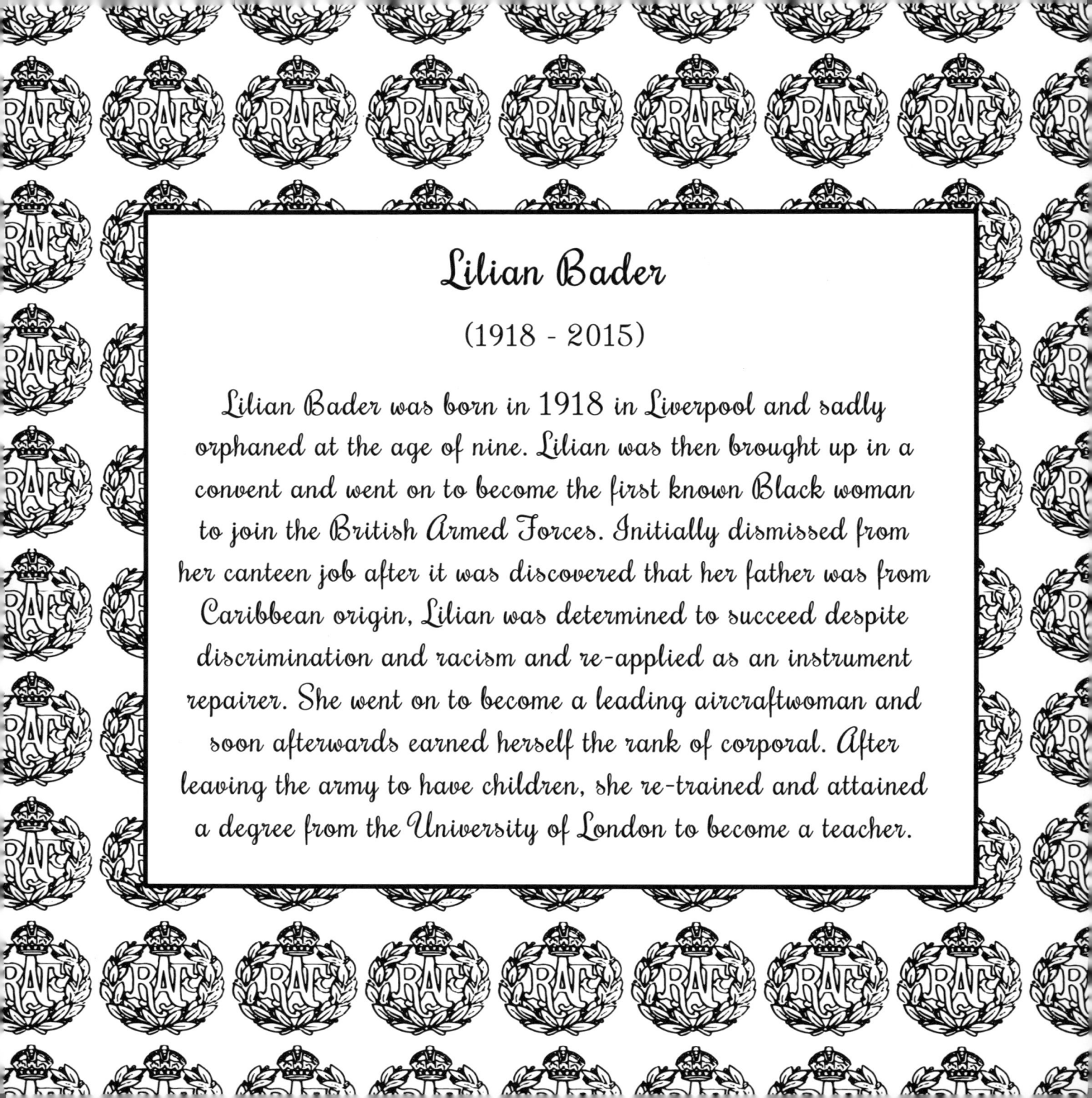

Lilian Bader

(1918 - 2015)

Lilian Bader was born in 1918 in Liverpool and sadly orphaned at the age of nine. Lilian was then brought up in a convent and went on to become the first known Black woman to join the British Armed Forces. Initially dismissed from her canteen job after it was discovered that her father was from Caribbean origin, Lilian was determined to succeed despite discrimination and racism and re-applied as an instrument repairer. She went on to become a leading aircraftwoman and soon afterwards earned herself the rank of corporal. After leaving the army to have children, she re-trained and attained a degree from the University of London to become a teacher.

Barbara Hepworth

(1903 - 1975)

Dame Barbara Hepworth DBE was one of the 20th century's most important artists. She is one of the few female artists of her generation to achieve international prominence. Her works exemplify Modernism and in particular modern sculpture and are celebrated on permanent display at the Hepworth Wakefield, a visual arts gallery and museum based in Barbara's birthplace of Wakefield, West Yorkshire.

Lily Parr

(1905 - 1978)

Lilian Parr was a 6ft tall professional football player from St. Helens. She scored more than 1,000 goals during her 31 year playing career and reputedly had a harder shot than any male player. She had started out playing football with her brothers on waste ground, before playing for the St Helen's Ladies team, and from there she was talent spotted and recruited into the Dick, Kerr Ladies F.C. which was made up of workers from a munitions factory in Preston, Lancashire. During the First World War, the women's game had overshadowed that of the men's but an FA ban on women's matches from 1921 to 1971 affected the course of the women's game forever. Parr is an LGBT rights icon and in 2002, was the only woman to be included in the English Football Hall of Fame at the National Football Museum.

Leonora Cohen

(1873 - 1978)

Leonora Cohen OBE, was a Leeds born suffragette and trade unionist. She was known as the "Tower Suffragette" after smashing a display case in the Jewel House at the Tower of London and had acted as a bodyguard for the famous suffragette leader, Emmeline Pankhurst who founded the Women's Social and Political Union advocating "deeds, not words". Leonora and other suffragettes are known for enduring hunger strikes when imprisoned for their political activism. The actions of the brave suffragettes are recognised as crucial in finally achieving the right for women to vote in Britain in 1918. Leonora lived to the grand age of 105 and also contributed to the second wave of feminism in the 1970s.

Ivy Benson

(1913 - 1993)

Musician and bandleader Ivy Benson was a glamorous and gutsy woman from Leeds, who led an all female swing band, proving that women could be great musicians at a time when the main orchestras and bands in the UK were filled entirely with male musicians. Benson and her band rose to fame in the 1940s, and were top of the bill at venues such as the Palace Theatre in Manchester and the London Palladium. Ivy ran her band from 1939 to 1982, survived sexist attempts of sabotage as the BBC's resident house band and allowed hundreds of women including legendary trumpeter Gracie Cole the opportunity to become professional musicians. It is with thanks to Ivy, that today female and male musicians work alongside each other in harmony!